My Corner of Maine

Neal A. Parent

My Corner of Maine

Photographs by Neal Parent

Introduction by Jane Day

Library of Congress catalog card number: 82-71759
ISBN: 0-89272-145-6
Design: Anne Kilham
Composition: Camden Type 'n Graphics
Manufactured in the United States of America

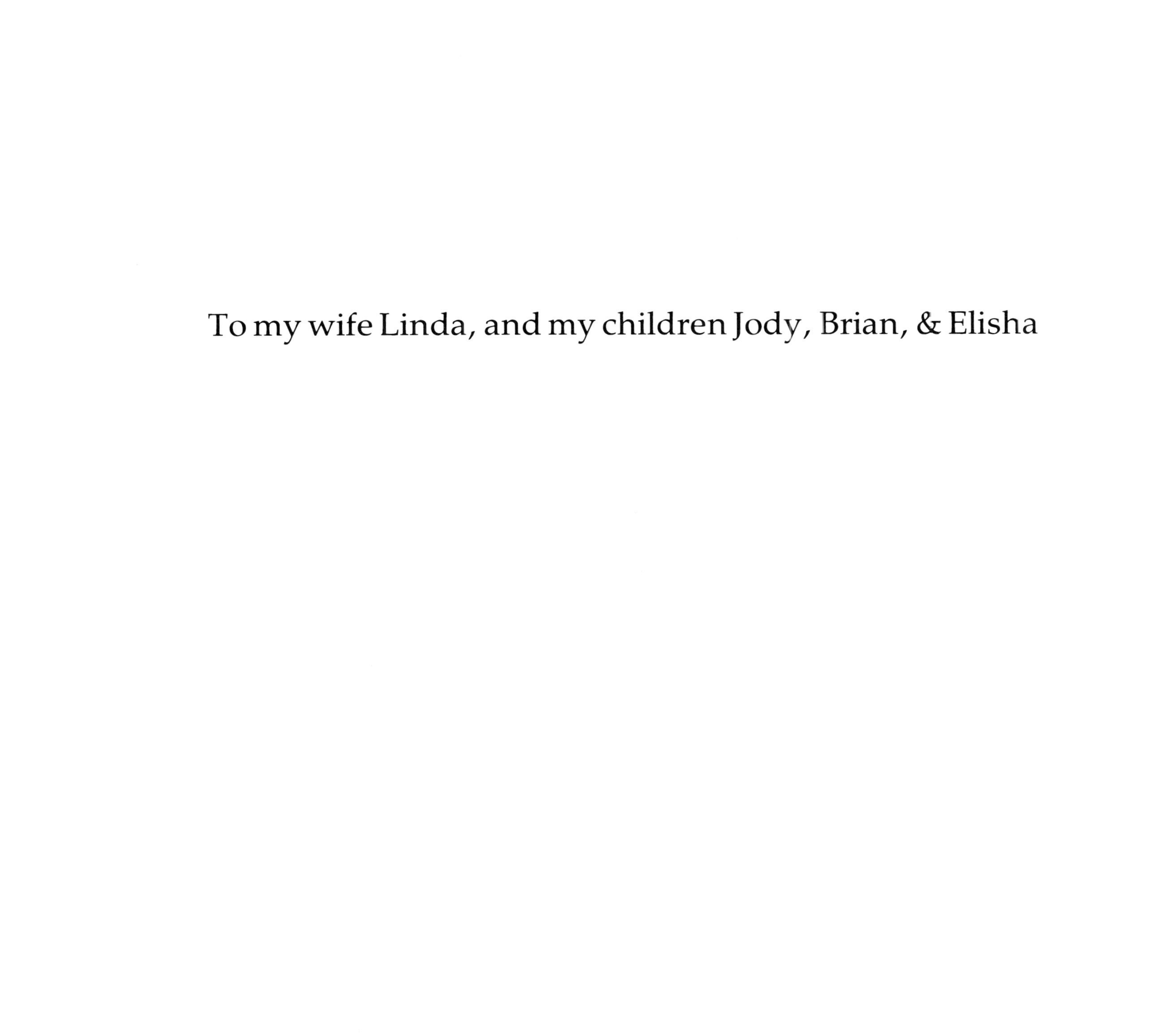

To my wife Linda, and my children Jody, Brian, & Elisha

It was raining that September day in 1975 when Neal Parent arrived in Camden — a Maine coast misting that settles damp in the bones, but not too cold for tenting out in the state park.

Neal stood in the doorway, reassuring me that he was set up just fine, all he needed was a couple of pots for cooking. And, thanks anyway, for offering the living room floor.

Neal had just been hired as the darkroom technician at the *Camden Herald*, the town's weekly newspaper, where I was editor. He had pitched his tent in the park while he looked for a house to rent for his family — his wife, Linda, and their children, Jody and Brian.

I remembered rainy campsites, coaxing fire out of wet wood to cook supper, and I understood his choice. Neal established his independence at the start, and I liked that.

When he found a house, Neal hired a U-Haul, drove to his home on Cape Cod for the weekend, and returned with his family and all their possessions. The quiet dispatch with which he handled logistics was a trait we all soon recognized. Now, as production manager of the *Camden Herald*, he continues to run the darkroom and take the photographs that have won him admirers across the country.

Neal had worked three years in the darkroom of a newspaper in Massachusetts, and was thoroughly familiar with processing and printing film. It was surprising, then, to learn that he did not own a camera, did not take pictures, and never had.

Whenever we reminisce about the "old days" at the *Camden Herald* before 1979, when the office was still located in the three-story brick building on Bay View Street, Neal insists that I am partly responsible for his first attempts at photography. We needed a scenic photo one week, and Neal says I urged him to borrow a camera and shoot a roll of film. He blew that roll somehow, but on his second try he came up with some good shots, including his first front-page photo in the *Herald*.

The photo disturbed me for some reason, perhaps because it was too typical.

But it ran — a gull standing sentinel beside the cannon at Lincolnville Beach. That photo still bothers me. But it was the beginning of the relationship between Neal Parent and a camera — a relationship that continues to develop and strengthen and refine itself.

Several years after he started photographing for the *Herald*, Neal got enough money ahead to buy his own camera. In the interim he had become familiar with cameras in the office: Minolta, Nikkormat, and a Honeywell Pentax that he later acquired in trade for some barn-building labor. This was the first camera he ever owned and it went everywhere with him until it was stolen from his car. Then he bought a Minolta, which he sold when he got a good buy on the 35mm Canon he now uses.

"I've learned that the camera doesn't make any difference," he told me recently. "I've seen people with $700 Nikons and I've seen people with a $75 Honeywell Spotmatic. It's knowing what you're holding. You've got to have an eye, a feeling for things, but you've got to know what you're using. You learn how to use your tools."

Neal does not own a lot of equipment or high-powered lenses. He believes you can do everything with the lens you have once you know how to use it. He owns only two lenses — a 50mm and a 135mm — and carries all his gear in a small leather case he found in a secondhand shop. He shoots almost exclusively in black-and-white, preferring it to color because, for him, it conveys more mood and feeling.

Photography is an extension of Neal's artistic ability, evident since he was a child. He excelled at drawing and painting, and studied art all through high school. During a four-year hitch in the Air Force Strategic Air command, he took a correspondence course in art. His work so attracted his commanding officers that Neal was pulled from his regular duty for a special three-month art project at the base. After the service, his hometown newspaper, the *Orleans Oracle*, hired him as an illustrator and cartoonist, a job that subsequently led to the paper's darkroom, where he got his introduction to processing and printing film.

"I don't have time now to sit down and draw or paint, but photography is a release for my creative side. I just have to paint or do something artistic, and photography has been that vent. I walk every inch of Camden, everywhere, snapping shots people wouldn't think of. I get very excited about it."

Neal's subjects are as varied as his interests and as wide as his ramblings. Animals, boats, people, reflections, patterns created by light, night shots — all are subjects. But more important than the subject is his feeling toward it: "I just get a gut feeling that it's a grabber. When I get in the darkroom, that's the big help to me. I know how to do my printing. I know what I saw, I remember it, and I have a good feeling about it."

Neal shoots quickly, making different exposures. He does not take hours setting up a shot or composing it. His picture is framed in his mind's eye before he picks up his camera. He anticipates the action, the light, and the change of season, which is why he is on hand at the flood tide storm, when the full moon rises just above the steeple of the Hope church, or as a youngster tests his kite in the early March wind.

"I've always studied people. I could sit on a park bench and watch people all day. You get pretty close to people if you watch them, and take their pictures, and talk to them. People get to know who you are. They respect you if your work is good, no matter what you do. I've got a good feeling about the people in Maine."

It is easy at any time for anyone with a camera in Camden to train it on the harbor. It was particularly easy at the *Herald* in those days, for our windows looked out on the public landing, the inner harbor, and past Wayfarer's point to the islands. While his film was drying, Neal would grab his camera and duck out the back door to rest his eyes, quiet his spirit, and more than likely shoot some film.

He was drawn to the harbor and the boats again and again — the bare masts and rigging of the schooners against the sky, the reflection of the sun on their plastic covers in the winter, and the regulars sunning on the green benches at the public landing in the spring.

"It's always different. It's never the same," he would say. And his photographs of the harbor became a twelve-month reflection of its seasons and moods.

When the high tide coincided with a southeast gale, Neal scrambled around the wharves and on the rooftops of buildings to photograph the scene. A pile of firewood floating between Jim Sharp's wharf and P. G. Willey's documents a flood stage story with an edge of humor.

Neal drove to work early from Searsmont — early enough to shoot the sunrise over the water or steal a silent portrait of an old boatbuilder with his morning mug up. Extremes of weather draw him like a magnet. He has come into the office dripping water after photographing a storm, his camera burrowed inside his jacket. When the mercury is fifteen below and a thirty-knot wind sends sea smoke

569·851

boiling over the harbor, half obscuring the schooners, Neal will plow through the snow along the seawall at the head of the harbor, shooting until his fingers are too stiff to snap the shutter.

As the months and seasons rolled into years, I found myself asking him whether we hadn't run that shot before, only to learn he had taken it that day. Neal knew it was time to expand his subject matter.

He began to look inland to the hills and woods and farmland of Searsmont where he and Linda had bought an old house with an FmHA loan. Elisha had been born by now, and she and Brian and Jody became the subjects for some of Neal's most appealing photos — the children curled up in their pajamas before bedtime, running with their dog down a country road, fishing at the edge of a marshy pond.

The commonplace, the everyday life of Maine people, assumed a timeless quality through Neal's lens, as revealed in the faces of his neighbors joking around the stove in the village store or studying the warrant from the back bench at town meeting.

One August morning as the mist was rising in the hollows, Neal stopped on his way to work and photographed blueberry rakers in a field on Route 173 — men, women and children, their backs bent over the low bushes. It was a picture that could have been made fifty years ago.

Setting, time of day, weather, all contribute to the quality that makes the commonplace memorable. For years a jeep pickup truck had been rusting in a field in Searsmont, the weeds and bramble tethering it to the ground. One summer morning about six o'clock, the sun touched the misty fields, silhouetting the derelict truck. "It seemed very beautiful," Neal recalls. The photo is one of his most popular.

Neal is partial to another field relic photo — a sturdy but crudely built high-wheeled wagon beside a sickle-bar hay mower. The outline of the Camden Hills forms the background, and the sky is dark with heavy, brooding clouds. The photo captures the sharpness and clarity of detail that precedes a storm. It also conveys a sense of expectation, created in part by the approaching blow but to a greater extent by the companionable cluster of wagon and mower that appear to have been left temporarily by a farmer who never returned.

The wagon and mower belonged to Orrie Buck, an old farmer in Hope who worked his fields with a team of horses. The road beside his aging barns and the giant oak was a peaceful place to stop and savor for a moment that steadfast life of an earlier time. This is what Neal was doing that day, showing visiting relatives the places he loved best in the communities surrounding his home. Orrie Buck had long gone. The weeds had grown up under his wagon. As Neal made his picture, the storm broke.

Neal came to Camden more by happenstance than by design. He had been to Maine and climbed Katahdin with his high school Sea Scout troop, but never was able to take the extended cruises aboard the scouts' ketch *Nauset*, which often made Camden a port of call. He was married and had two children before he ever saw the coast of Maine.

Neal and Lin were married in 1967 while he was still in the service. They were both twenty at the time, and had known each other since they were twelve. About nine years later, they came to Maine on a camping trip and stopped in Camden on their way down east. They liked it so much that they altered their return trip to swing through Camden again. Out of curiosity, Neal checked out the help wanted section of the *Camden Herald*, and there it was — the ad for a darkroom technician at the paper.

Neal went to the *Herald* immediately to apply. He looked around the darkroom, which was partitioned off at one end of the cellar, its walls painted a dingy gray over the bare foundation stones. Clipped by clothespins to wires strung across the room, negatives hung drying. Neal said he felt at home. From the start, he slipped into the *Herald* operation like an old pair of shoes.

It soon became apparent that Neal was handy. In spare moments he built a drying cabinet, another light table, some shelves. Before long, when something broke, our initial reaction was to open the door to the cellar stairs and holler for Neal. Almost anything from a stuck window to mechanical breakdown in one of the presses was within his capabilities.

The Photon, a computer typesetter that converted punched tape to print, was more complex. It required a trained serviceman, who came from Pennsylvania for repair sessions that often involved several days in Camden, with nights at a local motel included in the repair bill. As the frequency of Photon failures increased, the luxury of an out-of-state repairman became unthinkable.

The first time Neal was asked if he could fix the Photon, he asked innocently, "What is it?" But he could read the desperation in our eyes. Years back, he had managed an electronics shop in Massachusetts, and, so armed, he examined the Photon's innards. Deep within that web of wires something was not making contact. Like an infernal robot mocking our attempts to put out a newspaper, it spewed out garbled messages in caps instead of lower case, condensed Gothic instead of Bodoni Bold. Neal tracked the problem to its source and fixed it.

From that day on for as long as the *Herald* held onto it, Neal coaxed, cajoled, or cozened that machine into operation to get us through a working day. Then, on more weekends than most of us knew about (or that Neal cares to remember), he spent tedious hours replacing vital parts — hours that never were reflected in his paycheck.

When the *Herald* moved to newer quarters in the Highland Mill Mall, the Photon remained behind, and there is less demand now for Neal's skills as an emergency repairman. As production manager of the company, he is in charge of overall scheduling of newspaper and job printing work. And he is more serious about his photography than ever before.

Neal has won a couple of awards in the Maine Press Association photo contests, has had his own photo exhibit in a local bank and has published photos in *Small Boat Journal, Down East Magazine,* and *WoodenBoat.*

Last summer, Neal was asked to exhibit at Camden's annual outdoor art festival. It was his first big show and he was nervous. Not only that, he and Lin were too broke to afford the expense of matting and framing photographs, and setting up a booth. It was important enough to both of them, however, that they borrowed the money. Neal spent nights and weekends reprinting photos he had made over the years, fretted about their quality, and wondered whether anyone would buy them.

On the day of the show, he and Lin set up a few burlap-covered screens, hung up the photos, and were unable to move for the rest of the day because of the crowd of people that surrounded his exhibit. He sold all but a few prints and took orders for countless others — many long-held favorites by *Herald* readers.

Some of those photos are included in this book. Others date from his first years in Camden — the years of shooting with a borrowed camera whenever he could escape from the darkroom.

Neal continues to focus his lens on the mid-coast region, its land, and its people. His photographs are a human portrayal of the character of a place.

Camden, Maine
January 1982

Jane Day

WRESTLER
WRESTLER

Boats

"Boats are about the same as your friends. You wouldn't say you like one more than the other." Malcolm Brewer

Mobil
JOHN WANAMAKER

NOTARY PUBLIC

Animals

"I think I could turn and live with animals, they
are so placid and self-contained . . ."   Walt Whitman

Children

"If you don't believe in God, you'd better say your prayers." Brian Parent

PLEASE
TURN OUT THE
LIGHTS WHEN LEAVING.
THANK YOU.

Winter

"This woodstove is a full-time job. You wake up in the middle of the night and come down. It's something you do, keep the fire going . . ."

Jennie Pearse

Friends and Neighbors

"I like the working people of Maine . . . they maintain a marvelous ingenuity. There isn't the sort of industry here that makes people do routine things." Neil Welliver

MARINER

Cookies
CRIBBAGE
TOURNAMENT

Lunch & Supper Specials 11-7:30
England Clam Chowder 1.50 | 2.50
Rolls 3.25 Scallop Rolls 3.25
Turkey
SALAD Plate
dinner
Snow Crop

The Landing

Patterns

"The thing about Maine is what I call a quasi-Arctic atmosphere. It's incredibly crystal, incredibly clean. You can look for miles and see details." Neil Welliver